STECK-VAUGHN

Start Smart™
Connecting Learning to Life

Learning Skills

Written By

Julie Higgins

Consultants

Jim Ford
Training Specialist
Center for Literacy Studies
University of Tennessee
Knoxville, Tennessee

Daniele D. Flannery, Ph.D.
Associate Professor of Adult Education
Coordinator: Adult Education D.Ed. Program
The Pennsylvania State University
Capital Campus—Harrisburg

Barbara Tondre-El Zorkani
Educational Consultant
Adult and Workforce Education
Austin, Texas

STECK-VAUGHN
A Harcourt Company

www.steck-vaughn.com

Acknowledgments

Staff Credits

Executive Editor: Ellen Northcutt
Associate Editor: Sharon Sargent
Director of Design: Scott Huber
Associate Director of Design: Joyce Spicer
Designer: Jim Cauthron
Production Manager: Mychael Ferris
Production Coordinator: Paula Schumann
Image Services Coordinator: Ted Krause
Senior Technical Advisor: Alan Klemp
Electronic Production Specialist: David Hanshaw

Cover Illustration

Joan Cunningham

Photo Credits

P. 32 Sovfoto/Eastfoto/Picture Quest; p. 42 Tony Freeman/Photo Edit.
Additional photography by Comstock Royalty Free and Getty Images
Royalty Free.

ISBN 0-7398-6009-7

Start Smart is a trademark of Steck-Vaughn Company.
Copyright © 2003 Steck-Vaughn Company

Printed in the United States of America

2 3 4 5 6 7 8 9 0 MZ 08 07 06 05 04

Contents

To the Learner

You may not realize it, but you already have many years of experience as a successful learner. Were you born knowing how to drive a car, how to take care of a child, or how to do your job? Of course not. You have learned new skills throughout your life.

Learning is an active process. You can't just sit back and expect learning to happen to you. The good news is that *you* are in charge of your learning. You set the goals. You decide how to make the most of your learning opportunities. You will probably make some mistakes along the way, too. But don't worry. Making mistakes is an important part of learning.

As you work through this book be sure to:

- Write down your goals in the **Set Your Learning Goals** web on page 6. Your first step as an active learner is to decide your learning goals. Setting goals and checking your progress help you to stay motivated.
- As you read, check out the **Tips.** They provide a slightly different approach to the strategies.
- Complete the **Think About It** activities. These help you think about what you have learned. You'll also see the connection to everyday life.
- Review what you have learned by completing **What Works for You?** on page 48.

Set Your Learning Goals

You opened this book because you wanted to learn something. Maybe you are returning to school after several years. Getting your GED may be one of your learning goals. Of course, learning doesn't just happen in a classroom. You have learning opportunities in all areas of your life. You learn when you help a child with homework. You learn when you start a new job or take up a new sport.

What do you want to learn in each area of your life?

Look at the sample goals listed below.

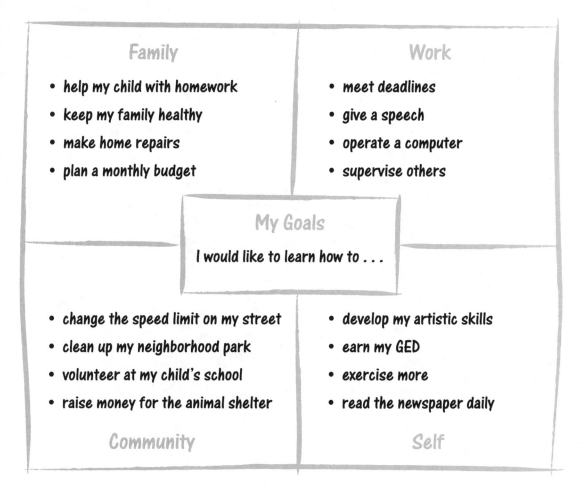

Family

- help my child with homework
- keep my family healthy
- make home repairs
- plan a monthly budget

Work

- meet deadlines
- give a speech
- operate a computer
- supervise others

My Goals

I would like to learn how to . . .

Community

- change the speed limit on my street
- clean up my neighborhood park
- volunteer at my child's school
- raise money for the animal shelter

Self

- develop my artistic skills
- earn my GED
- exercise more
- read the newspaper daily

Write your learning goals in the spaces below. Think about how becoming a better learner will affect your family, your work, your community, and yourself.

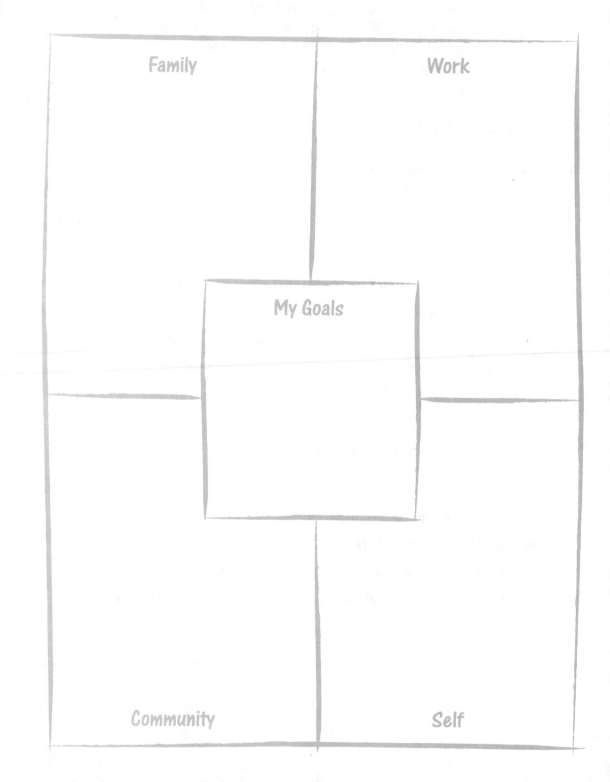

Family

Work

My Goals

Community

Self

Topic 1: Think About Learning

Learning is not attained by chance. It must be sought for with ardor (enthusiasm) and attended to with diligence (carefulness).

Abigail Adams, former first lady
(1744–1818)

Not everyone learns in the same way. Successful learners are people who take charge of their learning. They pay attention to the way they learn. It is important for you to take a closer look at the learning styles and learning places that work best for you.

In this section, you will learn how to:
- **recognize your learning style**
- **think about where you prefer to learn**

Many Learners, Many Styles
Raul, Sara, Jamal, Tina, and Joe are coworkers. One day their manager brings each of them a box containing a set of shelves to hold work supplies. But there's a catch. The shelves have to be assembled. The manager explains how to put the shelves together and then leaves. Here's what happens next.

- Raul opens his box and finds the instruction sheet. He studies the diagrams in the instructions. Then he builds his shelves.
- Sara ignores the instruction sheet. She uses what she remembers from the manager's explanation and builds her shelves.
- Jamal lays the shelf pieces out on the floor and picks them up one by one. He creates a solution as he builds his shelves.
- Tina and Joe team up to discuss possible ways to put the shelves together. They agree on a solution and assemble their shelves.

Did any of the workers do the job "the wrong way"? Of course not. Raul, Sara, Jamal, Tina, and Joe each successfully learned to build a set of shelves. However, the workers did use different *learning styles.*

TIP
If you are not succeeding with the learning style you are using, try out another style.

Strategy 1: **Learning Styles**

Every one of us has preferred learning styles. We each like to get and learn new information in certain ways. Knowing your own learning style can help you take charge of your learning.

Different situations may require the use of different learning styles. For example, if there had been no instruction sheet, Raul would have had to try another way. As you work toward your learning goals, you will probably have to use more than one style. Part of becoming a successful learner is expanding your ability to use a variety of learning styles.

Learning Through the Senses

There are many learning styles. The list below describes three of the most common learning styles. Notice that each of the styles is connected to one of the senses (sight, hearing, touch).

Visual (VI•zhu•ul): People who use the visual learning style rely strongly on their sense of sight. They prefer to learn by looking at drawings, diagrams, and illustrations. They learn by making mental pictures of information. Visual learners also learn by watching demonstrations.

Auditory (AW•di•tor•ee): People who use the auditory learning style rely strongly on their sense of hearing. They prefer to learn by listening. They also learn information by participating in group discussions and study groups. Auditory learners learn by asking questions and listening to the answers.

Kinesthetic (ki•nes•THEH•tik): People who use the kinesthetic learning style rely strongly on their sense of touch. They prefer to learn by handling objects and moving around. They learn information by making models and through physical practice.

Try It Yourself

Re-read the story of Raul, Sara, Jamal, Tina, and Joe on page 7. How did they learn? Divide them into visual, auditory, and kinesthetic learners. Explain your choices.

Learning Style	Name(s)	Why?
Visual		
Auditory		
Kinesthetic		

What is Your Learning Style?

Think of something you do well. It could be a hobby, a job skill, a sport, a creative talent, or an activity shared with friends. Try to remember when you first started doing it.

How did you learn?

....

Did you try it yourself?

....

Did you read about it?

....

Did you go to a class?

....

Did you watch a video?

....

Did you ask someone to show you?

....

TIP
Mistakes are an important part of learning. Be patient and keep trying!

Did you try something else?

....

Perhaps the first way you tried to learn didn't work. Why not?

....

....

....

In the end, what helped you the most? Do you seem to be a visual learner, an auditory learner, or a kinesthetic learner?

Work with a Partner

Share your answers to these questions with a partner. Describe your discussion on the lines below.

My experience with learning:

....

....

....

My partner's experience with learning:

....

....

....

How are your experiences similar? How are they different?

....

....

....

Think About It

How does your learning style affect your relationships with others?

....

....

....

Strategy 2: Learning Places

Now you have a better idea about *how* you prefer to learn. It's time to think about *where* you prefer to learn. Each learner will find certain learning places easier to work in. Sometimes you can control your learning place; sometimes you can't. The first step in creating an ideal place for your learning is to identify your needs.

Try It Yourself

Check (✓) all of the items that apply to you.

.... I ask someone to explain when I don't understand.

.... I want to have books nearby to look up information.

.... I like to talk about what I'm learning.

.... I like to move around when I work and study.

.... I prefer to learn by myself.

.... I prefer to learn with others.

.... I have more energy in the morning.

.... I have more energy in the afternoon.

.... I have more energy in the evening.

.... I can concentrate during one long study session.

.... I prefer to have several shorter study sessions.

.... I can study where it's noisy.

.... I need a quiet place to study.

Explain how well each learning place listed below and on the next page would meet your needs. Could a study group meet there? Would discussions disturb others around you? Are teachers or reference books available? Is the place available at the time of day when you have energy for studying? Would it be difficult to go there more than once a day? Is it noisy?

1. A library or reading room

....

....

2. Your living room couch

....

....

3. Your kitchen or dining room table

....

....

4. An empty classroom at a school or house of worship

....

....

5. A spare desk at your place of work

....

....

6. A room at a community center

....

....

7. A booth in a coffee shop

....

....

8. Your bedroom

....

....

Work with a Group

Discuss your results with two or three classmates. Talk about specific experiences. Compare your ideal learning places and then share with the class.

Now you know what the best learning conditions are for you. When you are studying in the right environment, your ability to learn increases.

Try It Yourself

Describe or draw your ideal learning place.

What steps can you take to make this a place for yourself? Check (✓) any that apply.

.... Check the hours when it's available.

.... Rearrange furniture and organize the place.

.... Inform family, roommates, or co-workers you will be using the space.

.... Get permission to use it.

.... Other steps. Explain. ....

....

> **TIP**
> *When you reach a stopping point in your study session, have a healthy snack. You'll return to your studies refreshed.*

 Think About It

How are you going to take charge of your learning?

....

Look at the goals you set on page 6. Note your progress for each of your goals. If you've achieved a goal, put a check next to it and congratulate yourself!

Topic 2: **Get Motivated to Learn**

First say to yourself what you would be; And then do what you have to do.

Epictetus, Greek philosopher
(50–120)

Some learning projects are more challenging than others. Successful learners are people who know how to overcome these challenges. Take a closer look at ways to motivate yourself and ways to stay motivated as you work toward your learning goals.

In this section, you will learn how to:
- **become an active learner**
- **better manage your time**
- **build a support system**
- **keep a learning journal**

Strategy 1: **Be an Active Learner**
You know what your learning goals are. You know how and where you are most likely to be a successful learner. Now don't just sit there—get motivated!

What is motivation? Motivation is the "push" that gets you started and keeps you rolling toward your learning goals. One way to get motivated is to become an *active learner*. The key to being an active learner is to find ways to become interested and stay interested in your learning. Active learning takes effort, but the payoff is worthwhile.

Take Charge of Your Learning
Motivated learners develop an "I-can-do-it" attitude. Here are some ways to become an active learner.

- Focus on how what you learn will help you reach your learning goals.
- Compare what you learn to what you already know. This helps the new information "stick" in your memory.

- Talk with others about what you learn.
- Right after class, try writing a paragraph about what you learned.
- Use a tape recorder to record the main points of a reading assignment.
- Write down questions you want to ask your teacher. Record the answers, too!
- Identify ways to use what you learn in your daily life.
- Use your new knowledge as soon as you can.

Work with a Group
Discuss some other ways to become an active learner. List your classmates' suggestions below. Share your suggestions with the class.

....

....

....

Learning Projects
Each learning project you try is a chance to move closer to your learning goals. When a project is large or takes a long time, you must stay motivated and remain an active learner throughout the whole project. You can do this by "checking in" at the beginning, middle, and end of the project. Ask yourself questions like those listed below.

> **TIP**
> *Keep a small notebook with you and write down things you need to remember in it.*

Questions at the Beginning of the Project
What are the requirements of the project?
When must the project be finished?
What do I already know?
What should I do first?
What resources do I need? *(Resources include books, photos, magazines, tools, people.)*

Questions at the Middle of the Project
What have I finished?
What do I still need to do?
Do I need to get help from anyone? Who?
Am I on track to complete my project on time?

Questions at the End of the Project
Have I met all the requirements of the project?
What would I do the same next time?
What would I do differently?

Let's look at an example of "checking in" during a learning project.

Learning Project: Write a five-paragraph essay about the invention of television. The essay is due in two weeks.

Beginning (beginning of week 1)

What are the requirements of the project? The essay must have five paragraphs. The topic is the invention of television. I must remember that the topic is NOT about any particular shows or actors.

When must the project be finished? The essay is due in two weeks.

What do I already know? List any facts I already know about the invention of television. Just get my ideas down. It does not have to be pretty yet.

What should I do first? Find the basic facts—who invented television; what the first television was like; where it was invented; when it was invented; and why it was invented. As I find this information, I should write it down.

What resources do I need? I started with general sources of information such as the entry "television" in an encyclopedia and the dictionary. Then I asked a reference librarian to show me how to find useful magazine articles and books.

TIP
Reference librarians are trained to help you find the information you need. Best of all, their help is free!

Midpoint (end of week 1)

What have I finished? I have written notes about the facts that will go into the essay.

What do I still need to do? Write the essay.

Do I need to get help from anyone? Who? I will not waste time feeling frustrated and alone. When I have trouble finding the facts I need, I will ask my teacher, a classmate, or a librarian for help.

Am I on track to complete my project on time? My time to work on the project is half over. I am halfway through with my work.

End (end of week 2)

Have I met all the requirements of the project? Yes! The essay has five paragraphs that describe the invention of television.

What would I do the same next time? I found helpful sources and people that I will use for my next project. I paid attention to the parts of the essay that my teacher praised.

What would I do differently? If I was unhappy with the way this
project turned out, I would take notes about what went wrong.
Then I will not make the same mistakes on my next project.

 Think About It
How will a "check-in" list inspire you to be a more active learner?

....

....

Strategy 2: Take Charge of Your Time

Few things are more frustrating than not having enough time.
Work, family, and other responsibilities compete for your time.
You probably already have a schedule. You have to be at work at
a certain time. Class meets at a certain time. Maybe you have to
take a child to school or daycare at a certain time. Time for learning
needs to be a regular part of your schedule, too.

Suppose you have to write a two-page report. The report is due in
ten days. Spend your scheduled learning time for the first five days
writing the first draft of the report. If you have questions, there is time
to find the answers. If you get stuck, there is time to find help. Then
you can use your scheduled learning time during the second five days
to finish the report. Putting a regular learning time on your schedule
eliminates frustration and last-minute panic. And, it is much easier to
stay motivated when things are going smoothly.

Work with a Group

Talk with two or three classmates about how you each find time for
learning. Do any of you have a regularly scheduled learning time?
List your ideas and suggestions.

....

....

....

Estimate How You Use Your Time

Most people don't have a very good idea of how they spend their
time. It just seems to go! The first step to taking charge of your
time is to keep track of how you use it.

TIP
Try to avoid distractions such as the television or telephone during your learning time.

TIP
Value your time. Learn to say "no" when there are too many demands on your time.

Try It Yourself

List the amount of time you think you spend each week on the following:

Family ....

Fun ....

Learning ....

Work ....

Other Activities ....

Track Your Time

Keeping track of your time for several days can help you understand how you spend your time and when you perform at your best. For one week, write down the things you do as you do them. Every time you change activities, whether opening mail, studying, making dinner, talking with a friend, or whatever, note the time of the change.

Try It Yourself

During the next week, keep track of how you spend your time on family, fun, learning, work, and other activities by completing this time chart.

Weekly Time Chart

Hour	Monday	Tuesday	Wednesday	Thursday	Friday	Saturday	Sunday
7:00							
8:00							
9:00							
10:00							
11:00							
12:00							
1:00							
2:00							
3:00							
4:00							
5:00							
6:00							
7:00							
8:00							
9:00							
10:00							
11:00							

Compare your chart to your estimates. After you complete the time chart, answer the following.

1. How accurately did you estimate how you use your time?

....

....

....

....

TIP
Decide what time of the day you get the most done and schedule your study time then.

2. Did anything surprise you about how you spend your time?

....

....

....

....

3. Did you have schedule conflicts? How did you resolve them? How could you avoid them in the future?

....

....

....

....

....

....

Now plan a week's schedule based on your time chart. Do not forget to include driving time. Leave some room for surprises. You do not have to schedule every minute. Make sure you allow some time for fun and winding down at the end of each day.

Weekly Time Chart

Hour	Monday	Tuesday	Wednesday	Thursday	Friday	Saturday	Sunday
7:00							
8:00							
9:00							
10:00							
11:00							
12:00							
1:00							
2:00							
3:00							
4:00							
5:00							
6:00							
7:00							
8:00							
9:00							
10:00							
11:00							

Think About It
How will better time management make you a better learner?

....

....

Strategy 3: **Build a Support System**

Every once in a while, learning is frustrating or discouraging. It can be hard to stay motivated all by yourself. Fortunately, you are not alone. Take some time to identify people and materials that support you and your learning goals.

TIP

Group interaction stimulates more ideas. Try finding solutions with a group of friends.

Create a Resource Web

What people or organizations are your biggest supporters? What materials can help you reach your learning goals? You can use a resource web to map out your support system.

Rashid is taking a business math class in the evenings. He made this resource web so he would know where to go to for help.

Me

my instructor
my wife
my supervisor
my classmate David

People Who Support Me

library
math center at the college
math tutoring on Tuesday
nights

Community Resources

my textbook
Basics of Business Math
    web page
online math tutorials
Business Focus magazine

Other Resources

Try It Yourself

It is important to locate and use all of your available resources. Create
a picture of your support system by completing the resource web
below. List the people who support you. Also list places to go in your
community for help and information. You'll also want to include
miscellaneous resources such as books to read and websites to visit.

People Who Support Me   **Other Resources**

Community Resources

Make a Contacts List

Once you have located your resources, you do not want to lose track
of them. These same resources can be useful in other learning
projects. Jot down their phone numbers or email addresses on a
contacts list for future reference.

Try It Yourself

Fill out a list with the names and contact information of people
and resources that support you at home, work, school, and in the
community. Refer to it when you need help, support, or motivation.

Work with a Partner

Talk about the following.

- How can you get motivated and stay motivated to learn?
- If you get frustrated, what can you do?
- If you want to talk about class, who can you call?

 Think About It

How can you keep from feeling overwhelmed by the number of things you have to do?

....

....

Strategy 4: Use a Learning Journal

Maria makes a New Year's resolution to improve her fitness. After checking with her doctor, she starts jogging. She keeps track of her progress in the chart below.

In addition to marking her distance and time, Maria notes how she feels.

Date	Distance	Time	Notes
1/2	1 mile	18 minutes	hard work: had to walk last 3 minutes
1/4	1 mile	15 minutes	pretty hard, but jogged the whole way
1/7	1 mile	13 minutes	still hard, but getting faster
1/10	1 mile	12 minutes	feel more comfortable, new shoes helped
1/11	1 mile	12 minutes	tried a different trail, too crowded
1/15	1 mile	10 minutes	regular trail; ready to try 1 1/2 miles next time

After several weeks, Maria looks back over her notes. She can see that she really is making progress toward her goal. Maria's notes about her jogging are called an *exercise journal.* The journal helps Maria stay motivated to keep jogging.

Successful learners keep track of their progress, too. Many find it helpful to keep a *learning journal.* Writing notes about your learning can help you organize your ideas. You can look back and see how much work you have done. It will be encouraging to see your list of new skills grow longer. You will have a record of past mistakes. But you will also have notes about how you fixed those mistakes. Your journal will help you stay motivated to reach your learning goals.

Get a notebook and start writing in it every day. List each new skill you learn. You can note your thoughts, attitudes, and feelings about your learning. Your journal is a good place to write down questions that you want to remember to ask your teacher. Make outlines of your plans for learning projects. And use the journal to keep track of what works for you. Be honest. If a learning project is not going well, use your journal to write about why. Then write about what you can do to make it better.

Here is an example of an entry in a learning journal. Of course, your journal may be a bit different. The important thing is that you record honestly your efforts to reach your learning goals. You may want to use colored pens and pencils or highlighters to make it more creative. You can draw diagrams or pictures if you choose.

Learning Goal:
Earn my GED

Today's Date:
9/20

Events:
Just finished first week of class

Thoughts, Attitudes, Feelings:
This is going to be a lot of work. I'm nervous, but excited, too.

How I'll Reach My Goal:
Set up a regular time and place to learn

Go to class two times each week

Organize study group with classmates Dan and Li

What Works/What Needs Changing:
Class will be very helpful/Need to move desk into bedroom so I can have quiet study place

New Skills:
How to make a schedule

Figured out my learning style

Questions to Ask at the Next Class:
Who is the author of the quotation at the beginning of this section? Why is this person important?

Try It Yourself

Begin your learning journal. Write any concerns you have about your learning skills. Then review the strategies for Topic 1 and Topic 2 on pages 8–25. Describe the strategy you think will help you the most with your concerns. Explain why. Try to be as specific as possible when you write.

 Think About It

How can writing help you visualize your success?

....

....

Look at the goals you set on page 6. Note your progress for each of your goals. If you've achieved a goal, put a check next to it and congratulate yourself!

Topic 3: **Explore Learning Skills**

Knowledge is power.

Francis Bacon, philosopher
(1561–1626)

Successful learners are not just "born that way." They are people who have mastered a certain set of learning skills. Successful learners use these skills to gather information, organize it, and store it in memory.

In this section, you will learn how to:
- *know the skills for learning*
- *recognize the steps for learning*
- *gather information*
- *organize information*
- *store information*

Strategy 1: **Skills for Learning**
Learning is much more than just memorizing information. As a child, you may have learned to sit in your seat, behave, and listen to the teacher. This is not, however, the role of an active learner any longer. Do your ideas about education help you to be an active, self-motivated learner or a passive learner?

> **TIP**
> *Use as many of your senses as you can while you are studying. You'll remember more.*

Try It Yourself
Read the following statements about learning. Do you agree or disagree with each statement? How does each statement fit in with what you already know?

- Learning means using your brain, your emotions, and all your senses.

....

....

- Learning means gathering knowledge, skills, and information.

....

....

- Learning means getting involved with the world around you.

....

....

- Learning means connecting new information to what you already know.

....

....

- Learning is going on all the time.

....

....

Complete the following statements based on your own experience.

I often feel .... when I am learning.

The sense I am most aware of using while I learn is

....

I enjoy learning about ....

I am not comfortable learning about ....

I learn best when I can ....

....

You may want to refer to your answers about your preferred learning style and place on pages 9 and 13.

Work with a Partner
Discuss your answers with a classmate. Record your discussion on the lines below.

....

....

....

Think About It
How can you be more of an active learner?

....

....

Strategy 2: Learning in Steps

Learning is a series of connected steps. You must

1. *Gather information* by using your senses (sight, hearing, touch, taste, smell).
2. *Organize information* by putting it in some kind of logical order. Take the time to organize what you are trying to learn. The payoff is enormous. Your brain has a *much easier* time working with organized information.
3. *Store information* in a way that lets you recall it correctly and use it later.

Learning skills are the tools you will use to complete each step successfully. The chart below shows the three steps of the learning process and the learning skills that will help you with each step.

Learning skills that help you Gather Information	Learning skills that help you Organize Information	Learning skills that help you Store Information
Observe the world around you	Decide which pieces of information are important	Pay attention
Use available sources	Identify relationships among pieces of information	Connect new information with what you already know
Ask questions	Put information in a logical order	Focus on understanding the meaning of new information
	Compare and contrast pieces of information	
	Recognize cause and effect among pieces of information	

All the learning skills listed above can be useful. Successful learners use a variety of learning skills. They know when a particular skill can be most helpful. How do you decide which learning skill to try? As you practice these skills, you will become more aware of when each is helpful. If one skill does not seem to do the job, try another.

Try It Yourself

Refer to the chart on page 29. Which of the three learning steps are you engaged in as you read this book?

....

Which learning skills are you using?

....

 Think About It

How have your feelings affected your learning in the past?

....

....

Strategy 3: Gather Information

The first step in learning is to gather information. Three learning skills that can help you gather information are:

- observing the world around you
- using available sources
- asking questions

Observe the World Around You

Use all your senses to gather information. Although you may rely mostly on sight, do not forget to pay attention to the things you hear, smell, touch, and taste. Your senses provide you with a lot of information.

Try It Yourself

Describe how you might make observations with each of your senses while learning to cook.

....

....

....

TIP

Make a checklist of what you need to know. Use it to decide what types of sources you need.

Use Available Sources

Gathering information from available sources may include going to a library or bookstore, visiting a museum, attending a performance, or logging on to the Internet. Knowing where to find information is an important skill.

Try It Yourself

The chart below describes various sources and the kinds of information you can find in them. Complete the chart by filling in the blanks with your own examples of how you use these resources. Do not forget to include examples from home or work.

Source	Examples of How I Use This Resource
Dictionary	I look up the meaning and spelling of words.
Encyclopedia	
Atlas	
Newspaper	
Internet	

Work With a Partner

Make a list of two or three possible sources of information about eating healthy meals.

....

....

....

....

Ask Questions

A person who writes about the day's news is called a reporter. A reporter gathers information about the news by asking questions. He or she often starts by asking these six questions:

You can use these questions to gather information, too. Read the following article.

NBC Finds Success with Olympics

NEW YORK — On Monday, NBC announced that its average prime-time rating for Winter Olympics coverage from Salt Lake City is 18.3. This is well above the promised 17.9. It beats the average for CBS's coverage of the Winter games in 1998 in Nagano.

A rating of 18.3 is very strong for the networks regardless of the Olympic games. Over the past few years, the networks (NBC, ABC, and CBS) have seen a sag in their viewership during prime time. According to NBC, its Olympic prime-time average is 138% higher than average prime time.

Officials at NBC cite the Salt Lake City location as one reason for increased ratings. A United States location means more live coverage is possible.

Source: *USA Today*, February 21, 2002

Try It Yourself
Use information from the article to answer each question.

Who made the announcement?
What did they announce?
Where were the Winter Olympics held in 2002?
When were ratings high?
Why do officials believe the 2002 ratings were higher than in 1998?
How does a rating of 18.3 compare to what was expected for 2002?

As you answer each question, you are gathering information from the article.

 ## Think About It
Which of your senses provides you with the most information?

....

....

Strategy 4: Organize Information

The second step in learning is to organize the information you have gathered. Organized information is much easier to understand and more likely to "stick" in your memory. Learning skills that can help you organize information are:

- deciding what is important
- identifying relationships
- creating a logical order
- comparing and contrasting
- recognizing cause and effect

Decide What is Important

Look at the information you have gathered. Some parts are more important than others. Some parts may not be important at all. Start organizing the information by deciding which pieces of information are necessary. One way to do this is to highlight or underline important parts of a book or article. Of course, you cannot do this in a library book! Another way to make important points stand out is to write them on note cards. Or, you could write an outline listing the most important information.

Work with a Partner

Talk with a partner about the advantages of each of these methods. List your answers below and share them with the class.

Method	Advantages
Highlight/Underline	....
Take Notes	....
Write an Outline	....

Identify Relationships

Another way to organize information is to identify the relationships among the ideas and facts. Often, making a diagram can help you see the relationships. For example, suppose you are learning about the bodies of water on Earth. You could make a list of the bodies of water you are studying.

> **TIP**
> *While reading, make a study guide to help you understand and remember specialized vocabulary.*

Bodies of water covered on test next Friday:

Oceans	Atlantic
Seas	Antarctic
Indian	Caspian
Pacific	Black
Arctic	

Can you look at this list and tell which of the bodies of water are seas? Is the Arctic a sea?

A better way to organize this information is to make a diagram. The diagram shows the *relationships* among the bodies of water.

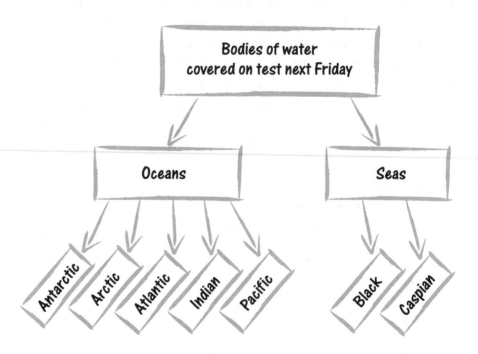

With the diagram, you can see that this test is over two types of bodies of water—oceans and seas. The diagram makes it easier to answer questions about bodies of water. The oceans are Antarctic, Arctic, Atlantic, Indian, and Pacific. The Arctic Ocean is not a sea.

Organizational Charts

An organizational chart is a common kind of relationship diagram. This chart identifies the relationships among employees at a company. That is, the diagram shows which workers report to which bosses.

This sample organizational chart shows information such as:
- three vice presidents report to the company president
- the director of accounting supervises the senior accountant

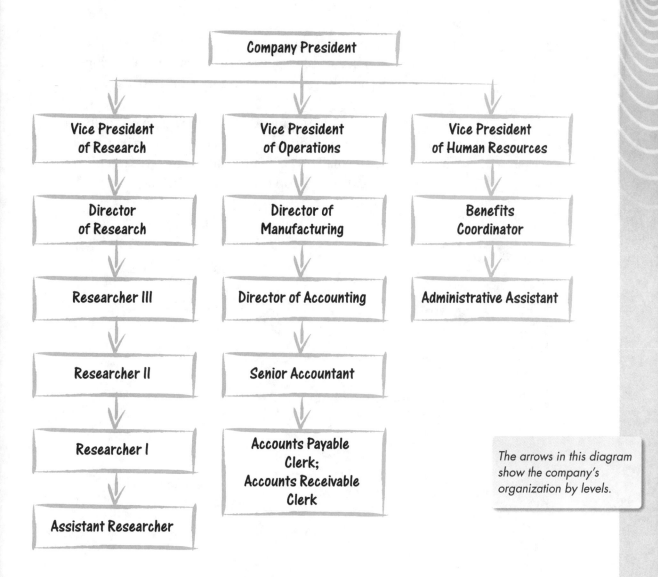

The arrows in this diagram show the company's organization by levels.

Try It Yourself

Draw an organizational chart of your workplace or another organization with which you are familiar. Start with yourself, your boss, and your boss's boss. Write two sentences that identify relationships among people on your chart.

....

....

Spider Maps

Spider maps, sometimes called mind maps, are another way to identify relationships among ideas. A spider map shows the relationships among a central topic, its subtopics, and the supporting details.

Why would you want to do this? Using a spider map can help you organize information before writing a paper. For a written paper, the central topic is the main idea of your paper. The central topic has several subtopics. Each subtopic has details of its own.

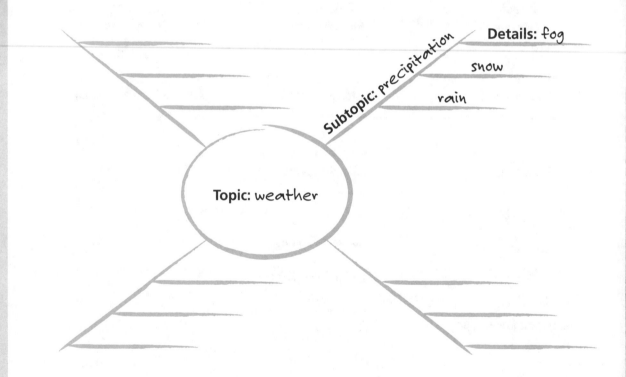

Work with a Partner

Find an article in a newspaper, magazine, or on the Internet. Read the article with a partner. Work together to make a spider map of the writer's ideas.

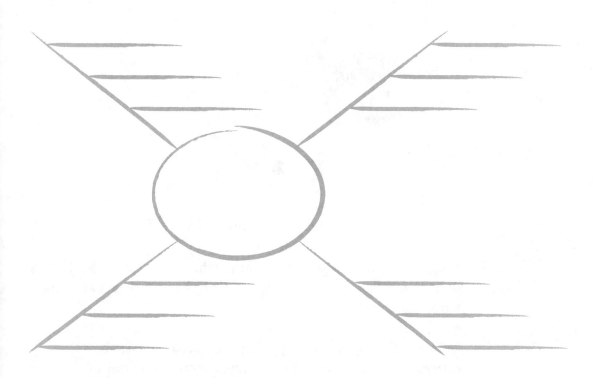

Create a Logical Order

For some learning assignments, the most important part is the order in which events happen. Look through the information you are about to organize. Words such as *first, second, next,* and *finally* provide clues to the order of events. Often things that happen in order are numbered. You will probably use this skill often, especially to organize information in history and science.

Putting information in a logical order is a very practical skill. You may know from your own experience that doing the steps of a task out of order can be inconvenient, or maybe even dangerous.

> **TIP**
> *The process of rearranging information helps you to understand and remember the material better.*

Try It Yourself

Practice understanding a logical order by reading the following selection about the life cycle of the gypsy moth.

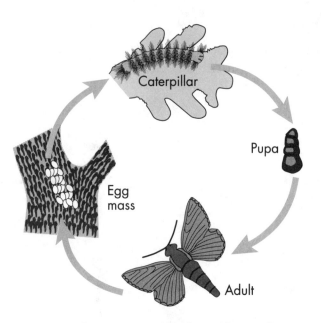

The Gypsy Moth's Life Cycle

1. Egg. Gypsy moth eggs are laid during the summer. Each female lays from 75 to 1,000 eggs in a clump called an egg mass. Egg masses are tan and slightly fuzzy.

2. Caterpillar. Gypsy moth eggs hatch into caterpillars. The caterpillars climb up trees to find leaves to eat. They grow to more than two inches long.

3. Pupa. During the pupa stage, the caterpillar encloses itself in a case for about two weeks. Its body changes into a moth.

4. Adult. When the pupa case breaks open, the adult moth comes out. Adult gypsy moths do not eat, so they do not live long. The female gives off a smell that attracts males. After mating, the male dies. The female lives long enough to lay eggs, and then she dies.

Answer these questions about the order of a gypsy moth's life cycle. Check your answers on page 39.

1. In the life cycle of a gypsy moth, which stage comes after the egg stage?

....

2. Which stage comes before the adult stage? ....

....

Answers

1. caterpillar
2. pupa

Compare and Contrast

Another way to organize information is to compare and contrast ideas. To *compare* ideas means to figure out how they are alike. To *contrast* ideas means to figure out how they are different.

By finding similarities between two ideas, you begin to see the connections between them. Finding the differences helps you identify what makes each idea unique.

The graphic organizer below shows how one person compared and contrasted two Mexican restaurants to help her decide where to throw a party.

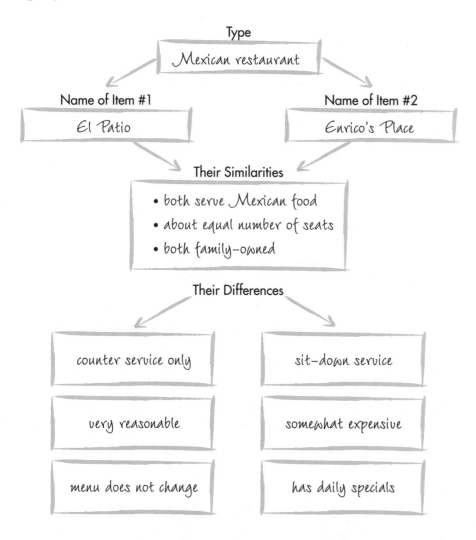

Type

Mexican restaurant

Name of Item #1

El Patio

Name of Item #2

Enrico's Place

Their Similarities

• both serve Mexican food
• about equal number of seats
• both family-owned

Their Differences

counter service only

sit-down service

very reasonable

somewhat expensive

menu does not change

has daily specials

Try It Yourself

Use the blank graphic organizer below to compare and contrast two things that interest you. The two things you compare and contrast should relate to your home, job, goals, or school. You might choose two neighborhoods, work tasks, classes, or something else.

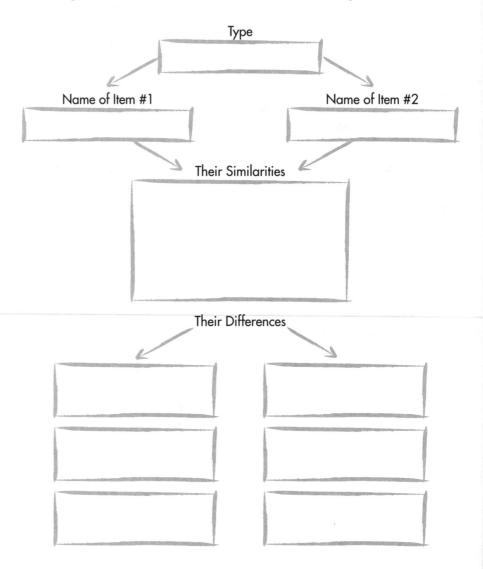

As you read material for various classes, you will need to be able to compare and contrast ideas. Words such as *in the same way, like,* and *similarly* can alert you to a comparison. Words such as *instead of, on the other hand,* and *unlike* may signal a contrast.

Try It Yourself
Read the following paragraph and answer the questions below.

Some physical activities, such as jogging, can put a lot of stress on joints. Sometimes, runners sprain a leg or ankle. A sprain is a joint injury in which the ligaments are stretched too far or torn. Ligaments are strong bands that connect bones at joints. A ligament stretches much like a rubber band. Unlike joggers, walkers rarely hurt their ligaments.

What comparison does the article make about ligaments?

....

What contrast does the article point out about walkers?

....

Recognize Cause and Effect
You can also organize information by recognizing cause-and-effect relationships. There are many situations in which one event (a cause) makes another event (an effect) happen. For example, missing the bus (cause) leads to being late for work (effect).

> **TIP**
> *The cause is the reason why the effect happened.*

When you study social studies and science, you will see many cause-and-effect relationships. As you read, watch for words such as *because, causes, is due to, effects, leads to, as a result, so, cost, therefore,* and *thus.* These words often signal cause-and-effect relationships.

Try It Yourself

As you read the article below, underline words that signal cause-and-effect relationships. The first one has already been done for you.

Consider the Costs

It is important to look at all the costs involved before deciding on a purchase. The cost of a new pair of shoes is not just the price of the shoes. For example, <u>as the result</u> of buying shoes, the shopper may have less money for a new winter coat. Good money managers know what the effect of most of their buying decisions will be.

The Riveras' budget allows only $140 a month for clothing, including shoes. Mr. Rivera needed work boots that cost $100. Mrs. Rivera needed shoes for a party. To stay within her family's budget, the pair she bought had to cost no more than $40. However, she chose to spend $75 on her shoes. Because of her choice, her family must spend less on something else to stay within the budget. As a result of her purchase, the family decided to play games at home one evening rather than go to the movies.

Did you underline "<u>Because</u> of her choice" and "<u>As a result</u> of her purchase"? The cause is Mrs. Rivera's buying more expensive shoes. The result is her family not going to the movies.

Try It Yourself

Answer the following question based on the "Consider the Costs" passage.

What would be an effect of ignoring the family's budget when deciding to buy something?

a. The shopper gets a better bargain.
b. The family might not have the money for something else it wants or needs.

The answer is b. Describe the thought process you used to answer the question.

....

....

Describe a cause-and-effect relationship with which you are familiar.

....

....

 Think About It
What do you notice first—how things are alike or how they are different?

....

....

Strategy 5: Store Information

The final step in learning is to store the organized information in your memory. Learning skills that can help you store information include:

- paying attention
- focusing on meaning
- making connections with what you know
- working to understand new ideas

Let's start with some basic information about how your memory works.

Using your memory goes beyond just memorizing information. Understanding how to use the power of your memory will give you more control over your learning.

Try It Yourself

Check your understanding of memory by reading the following statements. Mark each statement with a *T* if it is true or with an *F* if it is false.

.... **You either have a good memory or you don't.**

.... **Memory is where you keep information when you are not using it.**

.... **Memory is good only for learning facts and figures.**

.... **Memory happens regardless of your effort.**

All of the above statements are false. Read on for more information.

You either have a good memory or you don't. **False.**
You can learn ways to improve how you use your memory. This includes ways to get information into your memory and ways to retrieve it when you want.

Memory is where you keep information when you are not using it. **False.**
Your memory is more than just storage space. Your memory is active when you are doing many activities that do not relate directly to learning. You hold information in your memory that helps you do daily activities such as driving, cooking, or fixing something around the house.

TIP
Flash cards are a good tool for memorizing small bits of information.

Memory is good only for learning facts and figures. **False.**
Memory is part of all learning. You use memory to tell stories to your friends. You learn from past mistakes by remembering how events turned out in the past.

Memory happens regardless of your effort. **False.**
You do need to make an effort. Paying attention and focusing on what you want to remember will help. Reviewing study material at regular intervals will strengthen your learning.

Kinds of Memory

We have two kinds of memory: *short-term memory* and *long-term memory*. Short-term memory is also called *working memory* because this is where we begin working with information.

Short-term memory holds a limited amount of information for a limited time. An adult's short-term memory can hold from five to nine items at a time for ten to twenty seconds.

Examples of using short-term memory:
- dialing a phone number you just looked up
- understanding the paragraph you just read

As long as you repeat the information, it will stay in short-term memory. This method is useful for any bit of information you want to use and then forget, such as a phone number. However, this method does not help you store information in long-term memory.

Long-term memory consists of all the things we know. Information in your long-term memory is useful and meaningful to you. Information in your long-term memory is information you have learned.

Memory Systems

Short-term Memory	Long-term Memory
Holds information while you are using it	Stores information until you need it
Where you **understand** information	Where you **remember** information
Holds a **small** amount of information	Holds a **large** amount of information
Information is stored **quickly**	Information is stored **slowly**
Information is **forgotten quickly**	Information is **recalled slowly**

Short-term and long-term memory are related. In fact, information is constantly moving between the two. Information you use and hold in short-term memory may become part of your long-term memory. Information you retrieve from long-term memory goes into short-term memory while you use it.

TIP
Try writing ideas on paper as you learn. This leaves more room in short-term memory for you to think about what you are learning.

Work with a Partner
With your partner, identify how you use short-term and long-term memory in your daily life. Share your discussion with the class.

Research has shown that learners will remember:

10% of what they read.
20% of what they hear.
30% of what they see.
50% of what they see and hear.
70% of what they say.
90% of what they say and do.

What conclusion can you draw from this? Do you agree that you remember information better and longer when you do something with it? Use your own experience to support your opinion.

....

....

TIP

If you're having trouble memorizing, do something different for a while. The strategies may work better after a break.

Making something part of your memory requires you to take action. You put forth the effort in order to see the payoff. The learning skills that follow will help you store information in memory.

Pay Attention: Focus on the incoming information. Get rid of as many distractions as you can. For example, you will remember more of what you read if you do not watch television, talk on the phone, or cook supper while you read.

Focus on Meaning: You are more likely to remember information that is meaningful to you. Consider ways to use the new information in your daily life. For example, when you study math ask yourself, "How could I use this skill at home or in my work?" Think about how the new information touches your life. For example, when you read about history ask yourself, "How would this event have affected me personally if I had lived through it?"

Make Connections with What You Know: Some of what you learn is based on what you have already learned. A good way to remember new ideas is to link them to ideas that are already in your memory. Use what you already know to fill in any gaps in the information you are learning. Try comparing and contrasting new ideas with what you already know.

Work to Understand New Ideas: When you make the effort to learn something, you want to store it in your memory correctly. Make sure you understand new information so your memory will be accurate. Do not treat a lecture or reading assignment as just a string of words. Make sure you understand what it means. If you do not understand, ask questions! You are probably not the only one in class who does not understand. You do not necessarily have to ask your questions in front of your classmates. You might be able to talk with your teacher after class or you could ask another student. You could also do some more reading until you are clear about what you are trying to learn.

Try It Yourself

The chart below can help you practice the learning skills for storing information in memory. As you study, fill in the chart.

TOPIC:

How this information relates to me:

How I can use this information in my life:

How this information connects to what I already know:

Questions I have about this information:

Think About It

What do you do when you want to remember something?

....

....

Look at the goals you set on page 6. Note your progress for each of your goals. If you've achieved a goal, put a check next to it and congratulate yourself!

What Works for You?

Describe your learning style. How do you learn best?

How would you have approached a learning project before you read this book? Do you do anything differently now?

What was your biggest challenge as you worked through this book? How did you try to overcome this challenge?

How can you use the information from this book in your life?

What is your view of learning? Has your view of learning changed since you read this book? How has it changed?

Look at the goals you set on page 6. Have you met your goals? Answer the questions.

Which goals have you achieved so far?

Which goals do you want to work on?